EQUINE CARER

© 2024 Julie Dascoli

All rights reserved. No part of this book may be reproduced or transmitted in any form or by any means, electronic or mechanical, including photocopying, recording or by any information storage and retrieval system, without prior permission in writing from the publisher.

Published in 2024 by Amba Press, Melbourne, Australia.
www.ambapress.com.au

Previously published in 2015 by Hawker Brownlow Education.
This edition replaces all previous editions.

ISBN: 9781923116788 (pbk)
ISBN: 9781923116795 (ebk)

A catalogue record for this book is available from the National Library of Australia.

EQUINE CARER

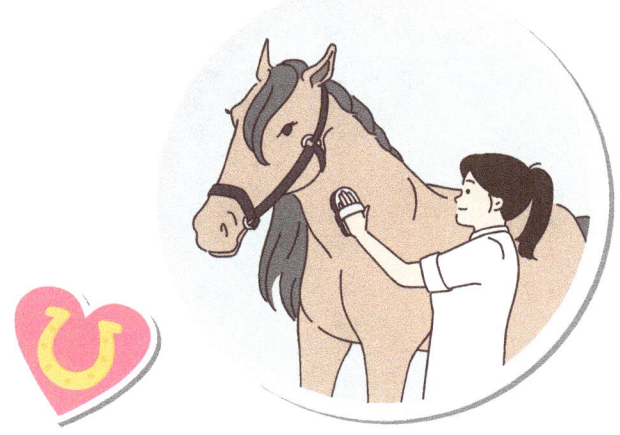

Written by Julie Dascoli

Photography by Laura Dascoli

Dear Reader,

Welcome to this volume of the *Real People Real Careers* series. I hope you'll enjoy learning all about Sam and her work as an equine service provider.

Before you read on, I'd like to say a few thank-yous to the people who helped to make this book possible.

Firstly, thank you to Laura Dascoli, who took the photographs you see in the book, and to Donna Dascoli, who provided initial editing and computer support services.

Secondly, my thanks to the staff and students in Years 4, 5 and 6 of the Mossgiel Park Primary School class of 2015 for their unwavering help and support.

And finally, I'm grateful to Sam herself, who generously gave up her time to help others learn about her profession – and to show them all the ways in which her job rules!

Happy reading!

Julie Dascoli

EQUINE CARER

I'm Sam and I'm an **equine** carer and service provider. Horses have been a passion for me since I was about five years old. At my local high school, I couldn't wait until I was in Year 10 so I could do work experience at my favourite horseriding school. I loved my placement and felt like I belonged there, so I was over the moon when they offered me an after-school job with them.

Even though I had to do all the really dirty jobs like feeding the horses and cleaning manure from the **stables** and paddocks, I didn't care – I just loved being around the horses.

I completed a **TAFE** course while I did Years 11 and 12. This meant that I was at school for three days a week and at **TAFE** the other two days studying for a certificate in **equine** studies. This type of study program is called **vocational training**, and it is offered for a variety of different subjects.

After Year 12, the riding school offered me full-time employment. I knew I wasn't going to be very well-paid, but it didn't bother me since I was so excited to get the job. I continued to perform **stable** duties, but I also began to learn how to be a riding coach. The school even paid for me to gain a coaching **qualification**!

I worked at the school for about four years, but while I loved the coaching aspect — especially working with children — the wages were not enough for me to pay for my car or look after my own horse, and they were definitely not enough for me to save money to buy a home one day.

On the advice of a friend, I decided to seek out a **traineeship** in business administration. I thought this would be beneficial to me as I aspire to one day own my own business. I applied for several positions and, after about six weeks of searching, acquired one in local government as a trainee administrator.

In a **traineeship**, the company pays for your training while you work for them. I completed my **traineeship** in two years, but I was still not happy. Sitting behind a desk doing paperwork all day was not my idea of a stimulating job.

After discussing the situation with my parents, I decided that I would try to open an **equine** services business. What I wanted to do was travel around and teach both adults and children to ride, plus I would train horses and provide any other services clients might need. I decided to do a course in **equine podiotherapy** to learn how to trim horses' **hooves**, as they grow continually like our toenails do.

I advertised on some free advertising sites and via social media, and friends helped me by spreading the word. Before I knew it, the phone started ringing with job offers from all over my local area.

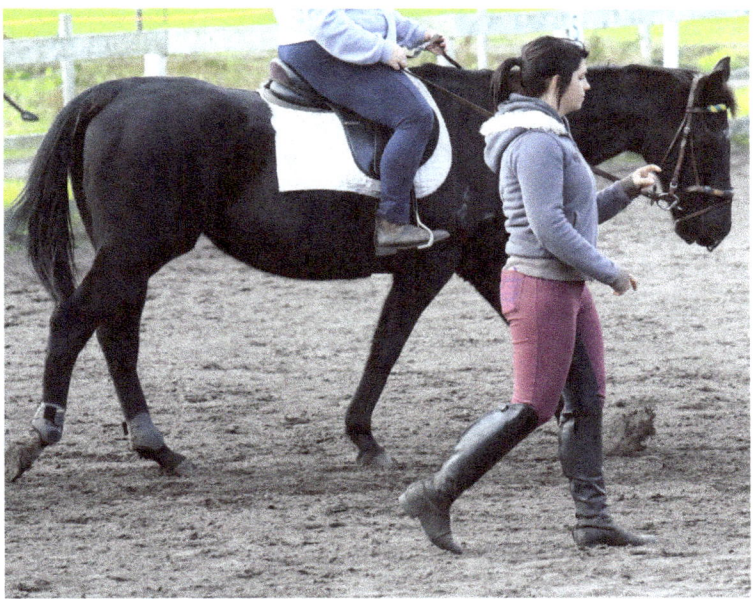

Clients were hiring me for all sorts of reasons: to teach people of all ages how to ride; to train clients' horses and get them ready for competitions; to give advice about nutrition; to perform hoof-trimming, grooming, **braiding** and **clipping**; and much, much more. It was very exciting to be working for myself.

The next step in my career is to work towards buying my own horseriding school. If I could achieve this, I could run my other services out of the school. That would be my dream job.

Interesting facts about my job

- I work 8–14 hours per day.
- I have about 40 clients.
- As I don't have a set lunchbreak, I eat between jobs.
- My dream job is to one day own my own riding school and **equine** services facility.
- I got my first horse when I was 17. I saved money from my part-time job to buy the horse.
- My favourite task is coaching.
- My least favourite task is getting up early.

What I wear to work

It's not compulsory for me to wear a uniform, as I work for myself, but I think it's good to have clothes just for work since I do get very dirty.

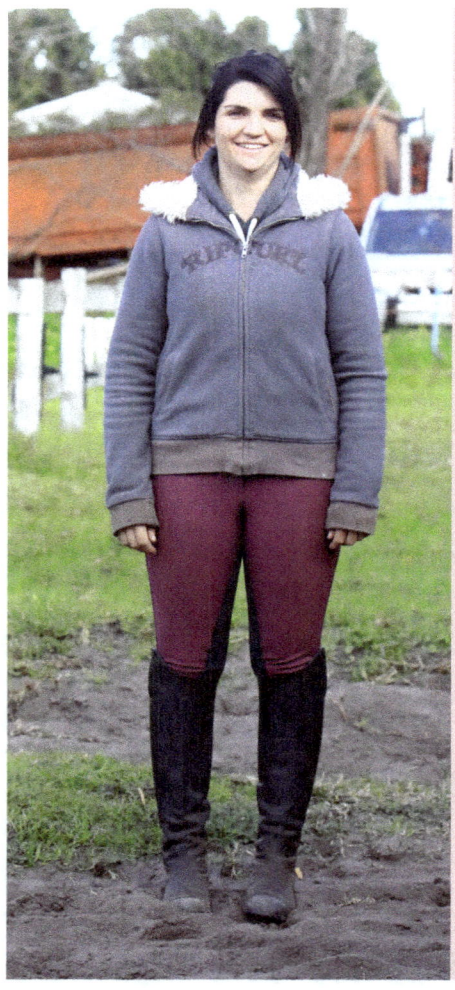

> I think it's good to have clothes just for work since I do get very dirty.

I have a T-shirt or polo shirt with my company logo on it, as this advertises my business name. I always wear special horseriding pants called jodhpurs along with leather riding boots, as I never know when I will be riding. When I am riding, I must put on a helmet that will keep my head safe if I fall off.

In summer, I wear a cap and sunscreen. When winter comes, I really rug up, as it can get very cold and wet outside. I wear a thick coat, scarf and beanie.

> I always wear special horseriding pants called jodhpurs along with leather riding boots, as I never know when I will be riding.

making lesson bookings on the go

What you need to do my job

- → You love horses.
- → You like science subjects.
- → You enjoy the outdoors.
- → You are **self-motivated**.
- → You are not afraid of getting muddy and dirty.

riding a quad bike

quad bike trailer for collecting horse manure

fixing fences

Related occupations

- → farrier
- → **equine** dentist
- → **equine** veterinarian
- → nutritionist
- → breeder
- → **equine** chiropractor
- → **equine** physiotherapist

Postscript

Sam has now found a riding school property with a house on it. She intends to live in the house and continue to do her **equine** services work from the property. People can go there to have lessons on their own horses or the school's horses.

view of the property

There are many jobs to do around the property. The horses need fresh water every day, and Sam uses the quad bike to take feed around to them. The fences and buildings need constant checking and maintaining, and Sam also has to pick up manure in order to keep the **stables** and paddocks clean.

hoof-trimming tools

hoof stand

Glossary

Braiding
A special type of plaiting that people do to a horse's mane — and sometimes its tail — in order to dress it up for competition. ***Braiding** is one of the services that Sam provides for people who want to show their horses but don't know how to present them.*

Clipping
The process in which a horse's coat is partially shaved for the winter. This is done to prevent skin infections, which can occur when a long winter coat causes a horse to sweat underneath its saddle. ***Clipping** is another service that Sam provides for her clients.*

Equine
Related to horses or other members of the horse family. *Sam works as an **equine** carer.*

Equine podiotherapy
The field of learning dedicated to trimming horses' **hooves**. *Sam did a course on **equine podiotherapy** so that she could offer hoofcare services to her clients.*

Hooves
A horse's feet and toenails combined. *Horses' **hooves** grow continually, just like human toenails.*

Qualification	The certificate, diploma or **degree** that proves you have completed training in a particular field. *Sam has completed several **qualifications**, including a coaching course, a **traineeship** and an **equine podiotherapy** course.*
Self-motivation	The ability to undertake a task or activity without another's supervision. *To become an **equine** carer like Sam, you need to have good **self-motivation**.*
Stable	A place where horses are housed. *Sam's first job at a local riding school involved cleaning out the **stables**.*
Traineeship	A course that requires you to work and study at the same time to obtain a **qualification**, usually over the course of two years. *Sam completed a **traineeship** in business administration.*
Vocational training	Education in a specific trade, the form of which usually differs from traditional academic study programs. ***Vocational training** is offered for a variety of different subjects.*

Other titles in this series

EQUINE CARER   PAGE 19

www.ingramcontent.com/pod-product-compliance
Lightning Source LLC
Chambersburg PA
CBHW070343120526
44590CB00017B/2997